Chocolate
Indulgences

Chocolate
Indulgences

Linda Collister

RYLAND
PETERS
& SMALL
LONDON NEW YORK

Designer Sarah Fraser

Commissioning Editor
Elsa Petersen-Schepelern

Editor Sharon Cochrane

Picture Research Emily Westlake

Production Gemma Moules

Art Director Gabriella Le Grazie

Publishing Director Alison Starling

Index Hilary Bird

First published in the United States in 2006
by Ryland Peters & Small, Inc.
519 Broadway, 5th Floor
New York, NY 10012
www.rylandpeters.com

10 9 8 7 6 5 4 3 2 1

Notes

All spoon measurements are level unless
otherwise specified.

All eggs are large unless otherwise
specified. Uncooked or partly cooked
eggs should not be served to the very
young, the very old, those with
compromised immune systems, or
to pregnant women.

Ovens should be preheated to the specified
temperature. If using a fan-assisted oven,
cooking times should be reduced according
to the manufacturer's instructions.

Library of Congress Cataloging-in-Publication
Data

Collister, Linda.
    Chocolate indulgences / Linda Collister.
        p. cm.
    Includes index.
    ISBN-13: 978-1-84172 -994-7
    ISBN-10: 1-84172-994-9
    1. Cookery (Chocolate) 2. Desserts. I. Title.
TX767.C5C6543 2006
641.6'374--dc22

                                                        2005013706

Printed in China

Contents

Introduction

It's said that women adore chocolate with the same passion that men feel for football. Eating really good chocolate is pure joy. Merely the smell is bewitching, and choosing which chocolate to buy is (for me) more fun than choosing a new pair of shoes.

The choice is expanding so rapidly that a "new" chocolate is lauded in specialty shops and top supermarkets practically every month. All the big names in the chocolate world sell tiny bars and squares of their most prestigious chocolates so you may try them before deciding on a favorite. Mine varies—I don't always cook with the same chocolate that I nibble after dinner. If I'm making brownies, for example, I will use something robust that will stand up to baking and to the other ingredients. But a simple and delicate mousse can showcase a "grand cru" chocolate with a complex, lingering flavor.

Using the best ingredients will make a difference to the taste and quality of any recipe, so pick the finest chocolate you like the taste of and can afford. The percentage of cocoa solids in the chocolate may appear on the label—60 to 70 percent is perfect. A higher percentage is not a guarantee of good flavor or quality. The chocolate must be perfectly balanced and shouldn't leave your mouth feeling greasy or astringent, nor should it have a harsh or burnt aftertaste.

So peel off the foil and break open the chocolate!

Sweet Treats

Chocolate is a perfect food, as wholesome as it is delicious,
a beneficent restorer of exhausted power.
Baron Justus von Liebig, German chemist, 1803–1873

When cool, the flat side of each Florentine is coated with dark or white chocolate, then "combed" to give a wavy pattern. At holiday time, replace the golden raisins in the mixture with crystallized fruits.

tiny florentines

6 tablespoons unsalted butter

3½ tablespoons corn syrup or golden syrup

3 tablespoons all-purpose flour

scant ½ cup chopped almonds

3 tablespoons chopped dried candied citrus peel

scant ½ cup golden raisins or candied fruits

½ cup candied cherries, chopped

4 oz. dark or white chocolate, or some of each, melted

2 cookie sheets lined with nonstick parchment paper

makes about 20

Put the butter and syrup in a medium, heavy saucepan and heat until melted. Stir in all the remaining ingredients except the chocolate.

Put teaspoons of the mixture onto the prepared cookie sheets, leaving room for them to spread. Flatten lightly, then bake in a preheated oven at 350°F for 7 to 8 minutes until light golden brown. Remove from the oven and let cool for 1 to 2 minutes, or until firm enough to transfer to a wire rack to cool completely.

When cool, coat the flat underside of each Florentine with melted chocolate and, using a serrated frosting spatula or a fork, make a wavy pattern in the chocolate. Let set, chocolate side up. Store in a cool place in an airtight container and eat within 1 week.

chocolate dials

To make the praline, put the nuts and sugar in a small, heavy saucepan and heat gently on top of the stove. Stir frequently with a wooden spoon until the sugar melts, then watch it carefully, stirring frequently, as it cooks and turns chestnut brown, and the nuts start to pop. Take care with this hot caramel, because splashes can burn you.

Lift the saucepan off the heat, quickly pour the mixture onto the oiled cookie sheet and, using a wooden spoon, spread it out evenly. Leave it until completely cold and set, then coarsely break up the praline with a rolling pin or in a food processor.

Put the chocolate in the top of a double boiler set over steaming but not boiling water and melt gently (do not let the bottom of the top pan touch the water). Remove the top pan from the heat and let cool for 2 minutes.

Drop 1 teaspoon of the chocolate onto the lined cookie sheet, then spread it out into a circle, about 3½ inches across. Press 2 hazelnut-size pieces of praline and 2 raisins into the chocolate. Repeat using the remaining chocolate, praline, and raisins.

Let set in a cool place or in the refrigerator, then peel off the paper. Store in an airtight container and eat within 1 week.

6 oz. dark chocolate, roughly chopped (about 1 cup)

⅓ cup large seedless raisins

praline

⅓ cup whole unblanched almonds

⅓ cup whole skinned hazelnuts

½ cup sugar

a cookie sheet, well oiled

a cookie sheet lined with nonstick parchment paper

makes about 20

chocolate truffles

3/4 cup plus 2 tablespoons
heavy cream

10 1/2 oz. dark chocolate,
finely chopped
(about 2 1/3 cups)

for coating

9 1/2 oz. dark or white
chocolate, roughly
chopped (about 2 cups)

a heaping 1/2 cup
finest-quality cocoa
powder, sifted

a pastry bag fitted with
a 1/2-inch plain tip
(optional)

several cookie sheets
lined with nonstick
parchment paper or
wax paper

makes 50

Put the cream in a saucepan and heat gently until boiling. Remove the pan from the heat and let cool for several minutes. Put the chopped chocolate in a heatproof bowl, then pour the hot cream* over it. Set aside for a couple of minutes. Stir gently until just smooth—do not over-mix at this stage. Let cool.

When the mixture is cool but not set, beat vigorously with a wooden spoon until very thick and much lighter in color and texture. Using a teaspoon or pastry bag, set marble-size pieces of the mixture onto the prepared cookie sheets. Chill in the refrigerator until very firm.

When ready to finish the truffles, put the roughly chopped chocolate in the top of a double boiler set over steaming but not boiling water and melt gently (do not let the bottom of the top pan touch the water). Remove the top pan from the heat.

Using 2 forks, dip each truffle into the chocolate until coated. Return the coated truffles to the lined cookie sheets and leave until the coating chocolate is almost set (if the truffles are very cold, this will be immediate). While the coating chocolate is still soft, roll the truffles in cocoa powder. Store in an airtight container in a cool place or in the refrigerator until ready to serve.

***Note** If you wish to add alcohol, do so before adding the cream. Try 3 tablespoons Drambuie, cognac, or orange liqueur.

Cakes & Cookies

The divine drink which builds up resistance and fights fatigue.
A cup of this precious drink permits man to walk
for a whole day without food.

Hernando Cortés (describing the hot chocolate drink), 1519

These cookies are my all-time favorites. For best results, use coarsely chopped dark chocolate rather than chocolate chips.

black & white cookies

1 stick unsalted butter, at room temperature

$^1/_2$ cup firmly packed light brown sugar

1 very large egg, beaten

6 tablespoons self-rising flour

$^1/_2$ teaspoon baking powder

a pinch of salt

$^1/_2$ teaspoon vanilla extract

$1^1/_2$ cups rolled oats

$6^1/_2$ oz. dark chocolate, chopped into chunks (about 1 cup)

several cookie sheets, buttered

makes about 24

Put the butter in a large mixing bowl and, using a wooden spoon or electric mixer, beat until creamy. Add the sugar and beat until light and creamy. Gradually beat in the egg, beating well after the last addition. Sift the flour, baking powder, and salt into the bowl, add the vanilla extract and oats, and stir well. When thoroughly mixed, stir in the chocolate chunks.

Put heaped teaspoons of the mixture onto the prepared cookie sheets, leaving room for them to spread. Bake in a preheated oven at 350°F for 12 to 15 minutes until golden and just firm. Remove from the oven and let cool on the trays for about 2 minutes or until firm enough to transfer to a wire rack. Let cool completely, then store in an airtight container.

The cookies are best eaten within 1 week, or can be frozen for up to 1 month.

double chocolate macaroons

Put the dark chocolate in the top of a double boiler set over steaming but not boiling water and melt gently (do not let the bottom of the top pan touch the water). Remove the top pan from the heat and stir until smooth. Let cool. Meanwhile, put the egg whites in a greasefree bowl and, using an electric mixer or beaters, beat until stiff peaks form. Gradually beat in the sugar to make a thick, glossy meringue. Using a large metal spoon, fold in the ground almonds, almond extract, and chocolate, and blend well. Put 1 tablespoon of the mixture onto a prepared cookie sheet and spread it out to a 2-inch-wide circle. Repeat with the rest of the mixture, leaving room for them to spread.

Bake in a preheated oven at 300°F for 30 minutes until just firm. Remove from the oven and let cool on the trays for 2 minutes or until firm enough to transfer to a wire rack. Let cool completely, then peel away the parchment paper.

To make the filling, heat the white chocolate and cream very gently in a small, heavy saucepan, stirring occasionally, until melted and smooth. Remove from the heat, let cool, then, using a wooden spoon, beat until thick and fluffy. Use to sandwich the macaroons together. Set aside for at least 1 hour before serving. Store in an airtight container.

3 oz. dark chocolate, chopped (about ½ cup)

2 extra large egg whites, at room temperature

1 cup sugar

4 oz. firmly packed slivered almonds (1 cup), finely ground in a food processor

2–3 drops almond extract

chocolate filling

4 oz. white chocolate, chopped (about ⅔ cup)

½ cup heavy cream

2 cookie sheets, lined with nonstick parchment paper

makes 8 pairs

chocolate crumble muffins

1¾ cups self-rising flour

a pinch of salt

⅓ cup plus 1 tablespoon sugar

6 tablespoons unsalted butter, chilled and cut into small pieces

3 oz. dark chocolate, grated or finely chopped (about ½ cup)

⅓ cup finely chopped unsalted nuts (optional)

2 tablespoons very finely chopped dried candied citrus peel

1 extra large egg

about ¾ cup light cream

chocolate chips or almonds, for decorating

a 12-cup muffin pan, lined with paper muffin cups or well buttered

makes 12

A cross between biscuits and shortcake, these muffins are rich, moist, and very crumbly. Eat them warm.

Sift the flour, salt, and sugar into a mixing bowl. Add the butter and, using the tips of your fingers, rub it in until the mixture resembles fine bread crumbs. Stir in the chocolate, nuts, if using, and citrus peel.

Break the egg into a glass measuring cup, then add enough cream to make 1 cup liquid. Add the mixture to the dry ingredients in the bowl and mix with a round-bladed knife until the dough comes together—it will be quite sticky.

Divide the dough equally between the prepared muffin cups, then decorate with chocolate chips or almonds.

Bake in a preheated oven at 425°F for 10 minutes, then reduce the heat to 350°F and bake for another 5 to 10 minutes or until golden brown and firm to the touch. Remove from the oven and let cool on a wire rack. When completely cold, store in an airtight container. The muffins are best eaten within 2 days, or can be frozen for up to 1 month.

fudge brownies

3½ oz. dark chocolate, finely chopped (about ½ cup)

1 stick plus 1 tablespoon unsalted butter, at room temperature

1⅓ cups sugar

1 teaspoon vanilla extract

2 extra large eggs, beaten

scant ¾ cup all-purpose flour

2 tablespoons unsweetened cocoa powder

a pinch of salt

1 cup pecan halves or walnut pieces

a cake pan, 8 inches square, buttered and bottom lined with parchment paper

makes 16

Put the chocolate in the top of a double boiler set over steaming but not boiling water and melt gently (do not let the bottom of the top pan touch the water). Remove the top pan from the heat and let cool while making the rest of the mixture.

Put the butter in a large mixing bowl and, using a wooden spoon or electric mixer, beat until soft and creamy. Add the sugar and vanilla extract and continue beating until the mixture is soft and fluffy. Gradually beat in the eggs.

Sift the flour, cocoa, and salt onto the mixture, then spoon the melted chocolate on top and gently stir together until thoroughly mixed. Stir in the nuts. Spoon the mixture into the prepared pan and level the surface. Bake in a preheated oven at 350°F for 30 to 35 minutes until a skewer inserted halfway between the sides of the pan and the center comes out clean—it is important that the center is just set but still slightly soft and not cake-like.

Let cool in the pan, then remove from the pan and cut into 16 squares. Eat warm or at room temperature. When cold, the brownies may be stored in an airtight container. The brownies are best eaten within 5 days, or can be frozen for up to 1 month.

cupcakes

³/₄ cup whole milk

2¹/₂ oz. dark chocolate, finely chopped (about ¹/₂ cup)

scant ²/₃ cup sugar

4 tablespoons unsalted butter, at room temperature

¹/₂ teaspoon vanilla extract

1 extra large egg, beaten

1¹/₂ cups self-rising flour

2 tablespoons chopped dark chocolate or chocolate chips

fudge frosting

3¹/₂ oz. dark chocolate, finely chopped (about ¹/₂ cup)

1 tablespoon corn syrup or golden syrup

2 tablespoons unsalted butter, at room temperature

a 12-cup muffin pan, lined with paper muffin cups

makes 12

Put the milk in a saucepan and heat until just scalding. Put the chocolate and one-third of the sugar in a bowl, pour the hot milk over the top, and stir until smooth. Let cool. Put the butter in a mixing bowl, then add the remaining sugar and vanilla extract. Using a wooden spoon, beat until light and fluffy, then gradually beat in the egg. Stir in the chocolate milk mixture alternately with the flour. Add the chopped chocolate or chocolate chips and stir to mix.

Spoon the mixture into the muffin cups until three-quarters full. Bake in a preheated oven at 350°F for 15 to 18 minutes until the cakes spring back when lightly pressed in the center. Let cool.

To make the fudge frosting, put the chocolate in the top of a double boiler set over steaming but not boiling water and melt gently (do not let the bottom of the top pan touch the water). Remove the top pan from the heat and stir in the corn syrup and butter. When smooth, let cool, stirring occasionally, until thick and on the point of setting. (If the mixture sets before you are ready to use it, gently melt it over very low heat.) Spread the frosting over the cooled cupcakes and let set before serving.

devil's food cake

Put the chopped chocolate, butter, sugar, and syrup in a heavy pan and melt over very low heat, stirring frequently. Remove the pan from the heat and let cool.

Sift the flour, cocoa, and baking soda into a mixing bowl and make a well in the center. Pour in the melted chocolate mixture, stir gently, then add the eggs, vanilla, and milk. Beat very gently with a wooden spoon until well mixed.

Spoon the mixture into the prepared pans and level the surface. Bake in a preheated oven at 325°F for 15 to 20 minutes until just firm to the touch. Let cool, then turn out of the pans.

To make the frosting and filling, put the dark and milk chocolates in the top of a double boiler set over steaming but not boiling water and melt gently (do not let the bottom of the top pan touch the water). Remove the top pan from the heat, stir gently until smooth, then beat in the sour cream. Leave it until very thick and spreadable.

Spread one-third of the frosting on top of one of the layers and set the second layer on top. Spread the remainder over the top and sides of the cake. Let set in a cool spot (not the fridge). Store in an airtight container and eat within 5 days.

3 oz. dark chocolate, chopped (about 1/2 cup)

1 stick butter

scant 1/2 cup dark brown sugar

1 tablespoon dark corn syrup

1 cup plus 2 tablespoons all-purpose flour

1/4 cup unsweetened cocoa powder

1/2 teaspoon baking soda

2 extra large eggs, beaten

1/2 teaspoon real vanilla extract

1/2 cup minus 1 tablespoon milk

frosting and filling

5 oz. dark chocolate, finely chopped (about 1 cup)

5 oz. milk chocolate, finely chopped (about 1 cup)

1 cup sour cream

2 round cake pans, 8 inches diameter, greased and lined with baking parchment

makes 1 cake

chocolate fruit & nut cake

1 cup large seedless raisins

¹/₂ cup candied cherries, cut in half

2 tablespoons rum, orange juice, or cold tea

2 sticks unsalted butter, at room temperature

1 cup plus 2 tablespoons sugar

4 extra large eggs, at room temperature, beaten

1$\frac{2}{3}$ cups all-purpose flour

1 tablespoon baking powder

a pinch of salt

1 cup ground almonds

3$\frac{1}{2}$ oz. dark chocolate, roughly chopped (about $\frac{1}{2}$ cup)

1 cup walnut pieces

a springform cake pan, 9 inches diameter, bottom lined with parchment paper

serves 10

Put the raisins, cherries, and rum (or orange juice or cold tea) in a small bowl, stir, then cover with plastic wrap and let soak for at least 2 hours, preferably overnight.

Put the butter in a mixing bowl and, using a wooden spoon or electric mixer, beat until creamy. Add the sugar and beat until light and fluffy. Gradually beat in the eggs. Sift the flour, baking powder, and salt onto the creamed mixture, add the ground almonds, and fold everything in using a large metal spoon. Add the dried fruit and rum mixture, the chopped chocolate, and walnuts, and stir gently until thoroughly blended. Spoon the mixture into the prepared pan and level the surface.

Bake in a preheated oven at 350°F for 1 to 1$\frac{1}{4}$ hours until the top is golden brown, firm to the touch, and a skewer inserted into the center comes out clean. Let the cake cool slightly in the pan, then invert onto a wire rack, remove the parchment paper, and let cool completely.

Wrap the cake in wax paper and keep overnight before cutting. Store in an airtight container. The cake is best eaten within 1 week, or can be frozen for up to 1 month.

pain d'épices au chocolat

Sift both the flours, salt, baking powder, and all the spices into a mixing bowl. Stir in the grated chocolate. Add the honey, egg yolks, and milk, and mix with a wooden spoon to make a thick, heavy cake mixture. Spoon the mixture into the prepared pan and level the surface. Bake immediately in a preheated oven at 350°F for about 45 minutes until the loaf turns golden brown and a skewer inserted into the center comes out clean. Invert onto a wire rack and remove the parchment paper.

As soon as the loaf is out of the oven, make the glaze. Put the chocolate, sugar, and milk in a small, heavy saucepan and heat gently, stirring, until the chocolate has melted. Bring to a boil, still stirring, let bubble for about 5 seconds, then remove from the heat. Pour, spoon, or brush the hot, thin glaze over the warm loaf and let it drip down the sides. Let the loaf cool completely before slicing. Store in an airtight container.

The cake is best eaten within 5 days, or the unglazed loaf can be frozen for up to 1 month.

*Note To make *quatre épices*, the late Jane Grigson mixed 7 parts of finely ground black pepper with 1 part each of ground cloves, ground ginger, and grated nutmeg.

1 1/2 cups all-purpose flour

3/4 cup rye flour

1/4 teaspoon salt

2 teaspoons baking powder

1/2 teaspoon ground cinnamon

1/2 teaspoon ground cloves

1/2 teaspoon quatre épices*

3 1/2 oz. dark chocolate, grated or finely chopped (about 1/2 cup)

3/4 cup plus 2 tablespoons clear honey

2 extra large egg yolks

5 tablespoons milk

chocolate glaze

2 oz. dark chocolate, chopped (about 1/3 cup)

2 tablespoons sugar

3 tablespoons milk

a loaf pan, 1 lb., buttered and bottom lined with parchment paper

makes 1 loaf

Desserts

If you are not feeling well, if you have not slept, chocolate will revive you. But you have no chocolate! I think of that again and again! My dear, how will you ever manage?

Marquise de Sévigné, French writer and lady of fashion, 1677

very rich chocolate brûlée

2 1/2 cups heavy cream

1 vanilla bean, split
lengthwise*

10 oz. dark chocolate,
chopped (about 2 cups)

4 extra large egg yolks

1/2 cup confectioners'
sugar, sifted

about 1/4 cup sugar,
for sprinkling

8 small soufflé dishes
or ramekins, 2/3 cup each

a roasting pan half-filled
with warm water

serves 8

Pour the cream into a heavy saucepan and add the vanilla bean. Heat gently until just too hot for a finger to bear. Cover the pan with a lid and let infuse for about 30 minutes.

Lift out the vanilla bean and, using the tip of a knife, scrape the seeds into the cream. Gently reheat the cream, then remove from the heat and stir in the chopped chocolate. When melted and smooth, let cool slightly.

Meanwhile, put the egg yolks and the confectioners' sugar in a mixing bowl, beat with a wooden spoon until well blended, then stir in the just-warm chocolate cream. Pour into the soufflé dishes, then stand the dishes in a water bath (a roasting pan half-filled with warm water). Cook in a preheated oven at 350°F for about 30 minutes until just firm. Remove the dishes from the water bath and let cool, then cover and chill overnight.

When ready to serve, heat the broiler to maximum and half-fill the water bath with ice cubes and water. Sprinkle the tops of the chocolate creams with sugar, then set the soufflé dishes in the icy water (this prevents the chocolate melting) and quickly flash under the broiler or with a blowtorch until the sugar melts and caramelizes. Eat within 1 hour.

*Note The vanilla bean can be replaced with 1 tablespoon dark rum—add it at the same time as the egg yolks.

chocolate waffles

1 1/2 cups all-purpose flour

a good pinch of salt

1/2 cup unsweetened
cocoa powder

2 teaspoons baking powder

3 1/2 tablespoons sugar

2 extra large eggs, separated

1 3/4 cups milk

1 teaspoon vanilla extract

3 tablespoons unsalted
butter, melted

confectioners' sugar,
for sprinkling

a waffle iron or electric
waffle maker, well buttered
(see recipe method)

**makes 10 waffles,
about 6 inches across**

Grease the waffle iron or electric waffle maker (consult the manufacturer's instructions if using for the first time), then heat. Depending on the type of waffle maker or waffle iron, it may be necessary to brush it well again with oil or melted butter, using a non-plastic brush.

Sift the flour, salt, cocoa, and baking powder into a mixing bowl, add the sugar, and make a well in the center. Add the egg yolks, milk, vanilla extract, and melted butter to the well and, using a whisk or beaters, beat until the liquids are just blended. Gradually beat the dry mixture into the liquid to make a thick, smooth batter.

Put the egg whites in a spotlessly clean, greasefree bowl and, using electric or egg beaters, beat until stiff peaks form. Using a large metal spoon, fold the egg whites into the batter until it looks evenly foamy—it is better to have streaks than to overmix at this point.

Using the large metal spoon, spoon in enough batter to fill the hot waffle iron, then close. Cook for 30 seconds over medium heat, then turn over the iron and cook the other side in the same way. Serve hot from the iron, sprinkled with plenty of confectioners' sugar. Repeat with the remaining batter mixture.

chocolate soufflé

Brush the soufflé dishes with a little melted butter, then sprinkle with sugar to give an even coating. Stand the dishes on a baking tray or in a roasting pan.

Put the chocolate in a heavy saucepan, pour in the cream, then set over very low heat and stir frequently until melted and smooth. Remove from the heat and stir in the egg yolks, one at a time, followed by the cognac or brandy.

Put the 5 egg whites in a spotlessly clean, greasefree bowl and, using an electric mixer or beaters, beat until stiff peaks form. Gradually beat in the sugar to give a glossy, stiff meringue. The chocolate mixture should feel comfortably warm to your finger, so gently reheat if necessary. Using a large metal spoon, add a little of the meringue to the chocolate mixture and mix thoroughly. This loosens the consistency, making it easier to incorporate the rest of the meringue. Pour the chocolate mixture on top of the remaining meringue and gently fold together until just blended.

Spoon or pour the mixture into the prepared soufflé dishes—the mixture should come to just below the rim. Bake in a preheated oven at 425°F for 8 to 10 minutes until barely set—the centers should be soft, and wobble when gently shaken. Sprinkle with confectioners' sugar and serve immediately.

about 1 tablespoon softened butter, plus a little sugar for the soufflé dishes

6 oz. dark chocolate, chopped (about 1 cup)

$^2/_3$ cup heavy cream

3 extra large eggs, separated

2 tablespoons cognac or brandy

2 large egg whites

3 tablespoons sugar

confectioners' sugar, for sprinkling

4 soufflé dishes, 1½ cups each, or 4 large coffee cups, buttered and sugared (see recipe method)

a baking tray or roasting pan

serves 4

This French classic relies on just three ingredients—
the finest chocolate you can find, the freshest eggs,
and unsalted butter. Serve in pretty glasses.

classic chocolate mousse

*3 oz. dark chocolate,
finely chopped (about $^1/_2$ cup)*

*2 tablespoons water, brandy,
or rum*

*2 teaspoons unsalted butter,
at room temperature*

3 extra large eggs, separated

4 serving bowls, coffee cups,
or glasses

serves 4

Put the chocolate and water, brandy, or rum in the top of a double boiler set over steaming but not boiling water and leave until just melted (do not let the bottom of the top pan touch the water). Remove the top pan from the heat and gently stir in the butter (it is important to melt the chocolate gently without letting it get too hot, and to stir as little as possible). Leave for 1 minute, then gently stir in the egg yolks, one at a time.

Put the egg whites in a spotlessly clean, greasefree bowl and, using an electric mixer or beaters, beat until stiff peaks form. Stir about one-quarter of the egg whites into the chocolate mixture to loosen it, then, using a large metal spoon, gently fold in the rest of the egg whites in 3 batches. Carefully spoon the mousse mixture into serving bowls, cups, or glasses, then chill in the refrigerator for 2 hours before serving. Best eaten within 12 hours.

nut & chocolate strudel

3/4 cup blanched almonds

1 cup shelled
unsalted pistachios

1 cup walnut pieces

5 tablespoons
unsalted butter

scant 1/2 cup firmly
packed light brown sugar

3 oz. dark chocolate,
chopped (about 1/2 cup)

7 oz. phyllo pastry
dough, thawed if frozen

whipped cream, for
serving (optional)

cinnamon syrup

1/2 cup sugar

1 cinnamon stick

1 teaspoon lemon juice

2 tablespoons honey

a large roasting pan,
well buttered

serves 6–8

Put all the nuts in a food processor and chop until they resemble coarse bread crumbs. Put the nuts in a heavy, dry skillet and stir over low heat until they just start to color. Because nuts scorch quickly, it's best to undercook slightly, rather than risk overcooking them. Remove from the heat and stir in the butter and sugar. Let cool, then mix in the chopped chocolate.

Put the phyllo pastry dough on a clean countertop and overlap the sheets to make a large rectangle about 36 x 24 inches. Sprinkle the nut and chocolate filling evenly over the phyllo, then carefully roll up. Arrange it in a horseshoe shape in the prepared roasting pan, tucking the ends under neatly. Bake in a preheated oven at 350°F for about 25 minutes or until the top is crisp and light golden brown. Remove from the oven and let cool in the pan while making the syrup.

To make the cinnamon syrup, put the sugar and a scant 1/2 cup water in a heavy saucepan and heat gently, stirring frequently, until dissolved. Bring to a boil, then add the cinnamon stick, lemon juice, and honey, and simmer for 10 minutes until syrupy. Let cool for 5 minutes, then remove the cinnamon stick and pour the warm syrup over the strudel. Let cool so the strudel can absorb the syrup, then cut into thick slices and serve with whipped cream, if using. Best eaten within 24 hours.

italian chocolate amaretto torta

4 oz. dark chocolate, chopped (about ²/₃ cup)

2 tablespoons amaretto liqueur (optional)

1 stick unsalted butter, at room temperature

¹/₂ cup plus 1 tablespoon sugar

3 extra large eggs, separated

2 oz. (about 10) amaretti cookies, crushed

¹/₂ cup all-purpose flour, sifted, plus extra for dusting

for serving

confectioners' sugar, for sprinkling

whipped cream

blueberries, raspberries, or baked apricots

a removable-bottomed cake pan, 8 inches diameter, buttered, bottom lined with parchment paper, then dusted with flour

serves 8

Put the chocolate and amaretto in the top of a double boiler set over steaming but not boiling water and leave until melted (do not let the bottom of the top pan touch the water). Remove the top pan from the heat, stir gently, and let cool.

Put the butter and the ¹/₂ cup sugar in a mixing bowl and, using a wooden spoon or electric mixer, beat until very light and fluffy. Beat in the egg yolks one at a time, then stir in the cooled chocolate. When thoroughly blended, use a large metal spoon to fold in the crushed cookies and flour.

Put the egg whites in a spotlessly clean, greasefree bowl and, using an electric mixer or beaters, beat until stiff peaks form. Beat in the remaining 1 tablespoon sugar to make a stiff, glossy meringue, then fold into the cake mixture in 3 batches.

Transfer the mixture to the prepared pan and bake in a preheated oven at 350°F for 30 to 35 minutes until just firm to the touch. Let cool in the pan for 10 minutes, then remove from the pan and transfer to a wire rack to cool.

Serve slightly warm or at room temperature, sprinkled with confectioners' sugar and with cream and fresh berries.

chocolate chip cheesecake

cracker crust

20 graham crackers, crushed

1 tablespoon unsweetened cocoa powder, plus extra for dusting (optional)

scant $\frac{1}{4}$ cup sugar

5 tablespoons unsalted butter, melted

chocolate filling

2$\frac{1}{4}$ cups cream cheese

1 teaspoon vanilla extract

$\frac{2}{3}$ cup sugar

3 large eggs, lightly beaten

1 cup plus 1 tablespoon sour cream

3$\frac{1}{2}$ oz. dark chocolate, finely chopped (about $\frac{1}{2}$ cup)

a springform pan, 9 inches diameter, well greased

a baking tray

serves 8

To make the crust, put the cracker crumbs in a bowl, mix in the cocoa and sugar, then stir in the melted butter. Tip into the prepared pan and press firmly onto the base and halfway up the sides with the back of a spoon. Chill in the refrigerator while making the filling.

Put the cream cheese, vanilla, and sugar in the bowl of an electric mixer and mix at low speed until very smooth. (You can use a wooden spoon instead, but it's hard work.) Gradually beat in the eggs, increasing the speed as the mixture softens. Finally, beat in the sour cream. Using a large metal spoon, stir in the chopped chocolate.

Pour the filling into the chilled cracker crust, set the pan on the baking tray, and bake in a preheated oven at 300°F for about 1$\frac{1}{4}$ hours or until just firm. The cheesecake will probably sink as it cools, then crack, so turn off the oven and leave the door slightly ajar. Leave the cheesecake to cool slowly in the falling temperature for about 1 hour. Remove from the oven and transfer the pan to a wire rack to let the cheesecake cool completely. Cover and chill in the refrigerator overnight before unclipping the pan. Serve dusted with cocoa powder, if liked. Best eaten within 4 days—store well covered in the refrigerator.

Use small saucepans or pretty heatproof bowls set over a warming tray or candle-warmers—and have lots of fun.

chocolate fondue

Put each type of chocolate in 3 separate coffee mugs which fit in the top pan of your double boiler. Set the pan over steaming but not boiling water and melt gently (do not let the bottom of the top pan touch the water).

Put the cream in another saucepan, bring to a boil, then add 3 tablespoons of the heated cream to each mug of melted chocolate and mix gently. If using white rum or Grand Marnier, add it to the white chocolate mixture.

Transfer the melted chocolate to 3 separate heatproof serving bowls and set them over the lowest possible heat on a warming tray in the center of the table. Cut the fruit at the table and immediately dip it into the melted chocolate fondues and eat.

4 oz. dark chocolate, chopped (about $^2/_3$ cup)

4 oz. white chocolate, chopped (about $^2/_3$ cup)

4 oz. milk chocolate, chopped (about $^2/_3$ cup)

$^2/_3$ cup heavy cream

1 tablespoon white rum or Grand Marnier (optional)

for serving

1 small pineapple

2 oranges

4 oz. strawberries (about 1 cup)

4 oz. cape gooseberries (about $^1/_2$ cup)

3 coffee mugs

serves 4–6

rich dark chocolate sauce

For a creamy sauce, use light cream instead of water or, for a flavored sauce, replace some of the water with a tablespoon or so of brandy, rum, or coffee liqueur.

4 oz. dark chocolate, finely chopped (about $2/3$ cup)

6 tablespoons unsalted butter, cut into small pieces

serves 4–6

Put the chopped chocolate, butter, and $1/2$ cup water in the top of a double boiler set over steaming but not boiling water (do not let the bottom of the top pan touch the water). Stir frequently until melted and very smooth.

Remove the top pan from the heat and stir the sauce well until glossy and slightly thickened. As it cools, it will become even thicker. Serve warm.

creamy chocolate sauce

A very quick, rich sauce for ice cream, profiteroles, and other desserts. Just before serving it can be flavored with rum, brandy, or coffee liqueur.

1/2 cup heavy cream

3 oz. dark chocolate, finely chopped (about 1/2 cup)

1/2 teaspoon vanilla extract

serves 4–6

Put the cream in a small, heavy saucepan and heat gently, stirring frequently. When the cream comes to a boil, remove from the heat. Let cool for 1 minute, then stir in the chopped chocolate. Stir gently until the sauce is smooth. Stir in the vanilla extract and serve immediately.

Ice Cream

Chocolate is a divine, celestial drink, the sweat of the stars,
the vital seed, divine nectar, the drink of the gods, panacea,
and universal medicine.

**Geronimo Piperni, quoted by Antonio Lavedán,
surgeon in the Spanish army, 1796**

deluxe chocolate ice cream

7 oz. dark chocolate, finely chopped (about 1 1/3 cups)

1 1/4 cups milk

1 large vanilla bean, split lengthwise

3 extra large egg yolks

1/3 cup sugar

3/4 cup heavy cream, well chilled

an ice cream maker or freezer-proof container

serves 4–6

Put the chocolate in a large bowl and set aside. Pour the milk into a heavy saucepan and add the vanilla bean. Heat slowly over low heat, stirring frequently, until the mixture is fairly hot—around 140°F—then remove from the heat, cover, and let it infuse for 15 to 20 minutes.

To make the custard, put the egg yolks and sugar in a bowl and mix well. Add the warm milk and mix thoroughly. Pour the mixture back into the saucepan and stir over low heat until the custard is thick enough to coat the back of a wooden spoon—don't let the mixture boil or it will curdle.

Remove the saucepan from the heat and discard the vanilla bean. Pour the custard onto the chopped chocolate and stir until smooth. Let cool, then cover and chill thoroughly. Put a bowl and whisk in the refrigerator to chill. When chilled, pour the cream into the cold bowl and, using the whisk, whip until soft peaks form. Stir in the chocolate custard.

Pour the mixture into an ice cream maker and churn until frozen. Eat immediately or store in the freezer. Alternatively, put the mixture in a freezer-proof container and freeze, removing it occasionally, stirring, and refreezing.

white chocolate ice cream

5½ oz. white chocolate,
finely chopped
(about 1 cup)

1 cup milk

1 cup heavy cream

1 vanilla bean, split
lengthwise

4 extra large egg yolks

⅓ cup sugar

an ice cream maker or
freezer-proof container

serves 4–6

Put the chocolate in a large bowl. Pour the milk and cream into a heavy saucepan, add the vanilla bean, and stir gently over low heat until the milk is fairly hot—around 140°F—then remove from the heat, cover, and let it infuse for 15 to 20 minutes.

To make the custard, put the egg yolks and sugar in a bowl and mix well. Add the warm milk and stir well. Pour the mixture back into the saucepan and stir over low heat until the custard is thick enough to coat the back of a wooden spoon—don't let the mixture boil or it will curdle.

Remove the saucepan from the heat, discard the vanilla bean, then let the custard cool for 2 minutes. Pour it onto the chopped chocolate and stir until smooth. Let cool, then cover and chill thoroughly in the refrigerator.

Pour the mixture into an ice cream maker and churn until frozen. Eat immediately or store in the freezer. Alternatively, put the mixture in a freezer-proof container and freeze, removing it occasionally, stirring, and refreezing.

pistachio and chocolate ice cream

Put the pistachios and 3 tablespoons of the cream in a food processor or blender and blend to a fine paste, scraping down the sides from time to time. Transfer the paste to a heavy saucepan and stir in the milk. Heat gently until almost boiling, stirring frequently, then remove from the heat, cover, and let it infuse for 15 to 20 minutes.

Put the egg yolks and sugar in a bowl and mix well. Pour in the pistachio milk and stir well. Pour the mixture back into the saucepan. Stir gently over low heat until the mixture thickens—don't let it boil or it will curdle. Remove the pan from the heat, pour the custard into a clean bowl, let cool, then chill thoroughly. Put a bowl and whisk into the refrigerator to chill.

When ready to churn, put the rest of the cream in the chilled bowl and, using the chilled whisk, whip until soft peaks form, then stir in the pistachio mixture and the chopped chocolate. Pour into an ice cream maker and churn until frozen. Eat immediately or store in the freezer. Alternatively, put the mixture in a freezer-proof container and freeze, removing it occasionally, stirring, and refreezing.

3/4 cup shelled unsalted pistachios

1 cup heavy cream, well chilled

1 1/4 cups milk

4 extra large egg yolks

1/2 cup sugar

3 oz. dark chocolate, finely chopped (about 1/2 cup)

an ice cream maker or freezer-proof container

serves 4–6

Conversion Charts

Weights and measures have been rounded up
or down slightly to make measuring easier.

Volume equivalents:

American	Metric	Imperial
1 teaspoon	5 ml	
1 tablespoon	15 ml	
¼ cup	60 ml	2 fl.oz.
⅓ cup	75 ml	2½ fl.oz.
½ cup	125 ml	4 fl.oz.
⅔ cup	150 ml	5 fl.oz. (¼ pint)
¾ cup	175 ml	6 fl.oz.
1 cup	250 ml	8 fl.oz.

Weight equivalents:

Imperial	Metric
1 oz.	25 g
2 oz.	50 g
3 oz.	75 g
4 oz.	125 g
5 oz.	150 g
6 oz.	175 g
7 oz.	200 g
8 oz. (½ lb.)	250 g
9 oz.	275 g
10 oz.	300 g
11 oz.	325 g
12 oz.	375 g
13 oz.	400 g
14 oz.	425 g
15 oz.	475 g
16 oz. (1 lb.)	500 g
2 lb.	1 kg

Oven temperatures:

110°C	(225°F)	Gas ¼
120°C	(250°F)	Gas ½
140°C	(275°F)	Gas 1
150°C	(300°F)	Gas 2
160°C	(325°F)	Gas 3
180°C	(350°F)	Gas 4
190°C	(375°F)	Gas 5
200°C	(400°F)	Gas 6
220°C	(425°F)	Gas 7
230°C	(450°F)	Gas 8
240°C	(475°F)	Gas 9

Measurements:

Inches	Cm
¼ inch	5 mm
½ inch	1 cm
¾ inch	1.5 cm
1 inch	2.5 cm
2 inches	5 cm
3 inches	7 cm
4 inches	10 cm
5 inches	12 cm
6 inches	15 cm
7 inches	18 cm
8 inches	20 cm
9 inches	23 cm
10 inches	25 cm
11 inches	28 cm
12 inches	30 cm

Index

Picture Credits

All photography by **Martin Brigdale**
unless specified below:

Tom Leighton
Page 7 top left, top right, and bottom right

William Lingwood
Pages 35, 55

Philip Webb
Pages 2–3, 4–5